CREATE
YOUR OWN

Flower
Tarot
Pack

A Complete Tarot
Pack to Colour

Sahar Huneidi-Palmer

ARCTURUS

To my beloved mum, Moutia, who spoke to plants, flowers, and birds. Thank you for instilling a love of nature within me.

Arcturus

This edition published in 2024 by Arcturus Publishing Limited
26/27 Bickels Yard, 151–153 Bermondsey Street,
London SE1 3HA

ISBN: 978-1-3988-1579-7
AD010370UK

Printed in China

Contents

INTRODUCTION 4

   The Origin Of Flower Reading 4

   The Minor And Major Arcana 5

The Suits 6

   Flower Definitions 6

   Preparing For A Flower Reading 6

   General Interpretations 6

   Tarot Flower Readings 7

   Table Of Correspondence Of The Minor Arcana 7

Tarot Spreads 8

   The Three-Card Spread 8

   A Sample Reading Using The Three-Card Spread 8

   The Celtic Cross Spread 9

   Sample Reading Using The Celtic Cross Spread 10

The Major Arcana 12

The Minor Arcana 22

   The Court Cards 22

THE CARDS FOR COLOURING 32

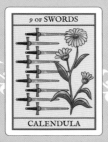

Introduction

THE TAROT BEGAN IN CHINA IN THE 9TH CENTURY AD, WHEN IT
WAS USED TO ENTERTAIN THE ROYAL FAMILY OF THE TANG DYNASTY.
WITH NO PICTURES OR NUMBERS, THE CARDS WERE PLAYED WITH
LIKE MONOPOLY MONEY AND WERE DIVIDED INTO FOUR SUITS. LATER,
THEY FEATURED CHARACTERS FROM A POPULAR NOVEL AT THE TIME —
AND QUICKLY GAINED POPULARITY SPREADING ACROSS THE CONTINENT.

They had reached the Islamic Mamluk Sultanate of Egypt by the 13th century, when titles and swords were added, as seen in the 17th-century Tarot of Marseilles. A full deck, known as the Topkapi, dating back to the 15th century and including 52 cards of four suits — polo sticks, coins, swords and cups — was unearthed in 1939 near Istanbul.

Two ladies have their cards read in a parlour in 19th-century France.

The cards arrived in Europe in the late 14th century via the Levant, where they were used for entertainment by the aristocracy. Titles were modified to reflect European royalty, and images were also included. Their popularity increased to the point where state religion regarded them as 'evils of idle play'. Around this period, religious images such as Angels, The Pope, Death and The Devil began to appear on playing cards. By the end of the 17th century, The Tarot featured Arabic numerals, images and names and were known as face cards or trump cards (major cards) – quite similar to the Tarot cards we know today.

The Origin of Flower Reading

Today, there are hundreds of Tarot designs and themes to pick from. Now, you can create your own Flower Tarot deck using your favourite colours.

Flower reading is an old art that uses symbolism, intuition, and flower knowledge to interpret messages. The person chooses a flower from a vase or a deck of cards with floral imagery. People are encouraged to choose the flower or card that 'speaks to them' or draws them.

Nature, flowers and herbs have always been revered by humans for their beauty and medicinal abilities. 'When you have just two pennies left in the world, purchase a loaf of bread with one and flowers with the other', says an ancient Chinese saying.

Floriography, or 'the language of flowers', was a popular Victorian obsession in which different plants and flowers were attributed different meanings. The majority of flowers conveyed positive sentiments such as friendship, faithfulness, dedication and love. Others were given more negative connotations, like rage, scorn, or apathy.

The Minor and Major Arcana

A standard Tarot deck is made up of 78 cards, 56 of which are split into four suits called the Minor Arcana. The remaining 22 cards are known as the Major Arcana. Arcana is a Latin term that means 'secret' or 'mystery', and it relates to the secret knowledge or wisdom that the Tarot reveals.

The Minor Arcana cards symbolize the four elements of fire, earth, air and water, as well as other traits: creativity, abundance, thoughts and emotions respectively — and reveal more details and timings in a tarot reading.

The major cards denote major life changes and transitions, depicting the stages of self-development, and are numbered from 0 to 21, beginning with The Fool at 0 and ending with The World at 21. The sequence varies slightly depending on the pack.

These cards from the Rider Waite Smith Tarot deck have been illustrated in a classic style and depict three of the Major Arcana cards.

THE SUITS

The Minor Arcana in a standard Tarot deck resembles a deck of playing cards and is divided into four suits. Each suit corresponds to a suit of playing cards: wands or batons (clubs), cups or chalices (hearts), swords (spades) and coins or pentacles (diamonds).

Each suit has four sets of cards, numbered 1 to 10, with the ace as the first card. Additionally, each suit has four court cards: King, Queen, Knight and Page.

FLOWER DEFINITIONS

A flower's appearance, colour or behaviour expresses its message. The Sunflower card, for example, is associated with The Sun. Sunflowers, like The Sun, are round, bright and life-giving. Working with the flower cards helps you strengthen your intuition, allowing your mind to receive intuitive messages. Flower readings are a fascinating way to solve life's mysteries and liven up any party or event!

PPREPARING FOR A FLOWER READING

Create your own ceremony for using and caring for your Tarot Flower pack. When not using them, store the cards in a cloth, pouch or box. Consulting the cards is similar to asking a personal confidante for advice. So, deepen your connection to them by being the only handler. Moreover, every now and again, use incense or a few drops of essential oils, or intention, to cleanse the cards from previous energies.

Whenever you begin a reading, mentally ask for guidance 'from the highest Source for the highest good' and shuffle the cards while focusing on your question or issue. If you are reading for someone else (the querent), request them to shuffle the pack before returning it to you to cut and place according to a spread.

Cut the pack in half or three piles, and then choose cards at random to lay out using your preferred spread (as shown on pages 8–11). Alternatively, spread the pack out on a table and draw the desired number of cards at random, arranging them according to the sequence of your chosen spread. If you are a beginner, you can start by using the Major Arcana on its own, and still receive meaningful insights.

General Interpretations

When several cards of the same colour or description appear in a spread, it indicates an underlying theme, emotion or thinking that may be impacting the situation. When the Major Arcana cards dominate a spread, it indicates larger forces at work; or that external influences may determine the outcome. When mainly Minor Arcana cards appear, the situation may be in the hands of the querent, as minor cards represent a person's own habits, feelings and thoughts.

Aces are associated with new beginnings and may suggest that the answer to a question is 'Yes'. Court cards might represent persons in our life who have the attributes associated with the cards, or they can represent qualities in ourselves.

There's no need to reverse any cards while shuffling, because each flower has a unique meaning that delivers its message. It is critical to remember that the Tarot cards indicate patterns at work in your life and your deepest self, rather than a mere prediction tool. You should go into the reading with humility, compassion and consideration for all individuals involved, including yourself. Never end the reading on a negative note.

Tarot Flower Readings

A flower reading requires the cards to be laid out in a spread, to understand their individual meaning, as well as their interpretation, according to their position. A spread helps you 'weave a story' to deliver a message or advice. There are numerous spread templates, ranging from simple to complex. In any spread, you can use the major cards on their own, or in combination with the minor cards. However, it is easier to begin with simple spreads that use the major cards only. As your confidence and understanding grows, you can start using more complex spreads or create your own.

Consider the meaning of each card, and look for a common meaning or message delivered by each flower. When you combine that with the position they fall in, you will have a wealth of information! Remember that a Tarot Flower reading is a combination of the meaning of each individual card and its interpretation based on where it falls in a spread. Your intuition will interpret the cards based on the 'story' told by the flower cards and where they fall in a spread. With practice, your readings will become more insightful as your intuition grows.

TABLE OF CORRESPONDENCE OF THE MINOR ARCANA

Suit	Element	Season/ Timing	Key Word	Qualities	Playing Cards Correspondence
WANDS	Fire	Spring	Ideas	Male aspect, inspiration, renewal, manifestation of ideas, growth, communication and self-expression.	♣
CUPS	Water	Summer	Emotions	Female aspect, emotions, creativity, happiness, love, intuition, acceptance, flow.	♥
SWORDS	Air	Autumn	Thoughts	Sharp mind, mental activity, intellect, logical thinking, decisions.	♠
PENTACLES	Earth	Winter	Finance	Money, material wealth, success, business, physical body, foundation, property.	♦

TAROT SPREADS

Choose a single card from your pack to obtain insight into an issue or incident in your life or to assist you in focusing and meditating. Alternatively, try one of the popular tarot spreads listed below to arrange the cards before a reading.

The three-card spread

This is one of the simplest spreads. Shuffle the cards while focusing on your question, and lay out three cards from left to right, face up. The first card represents the past, to the right of this is the second card, representing the present, and the final card, to its right, represents the future or the outcome.

A SAMPLE READING USING THE THREE-CARD SPREAD

The querent is a male in his late thirties. He had several failed relationships in the past, and is asking the cards about his love life in the future. He wants to know if a future relationship will bring him happiness. He has laid down the following cards:

Card 1: the past

The Moon – the Calla Lily represents his history and indicates confusion and illusion about former relationships. He didn't listen to his own intuition or feelings. Instead, he was needy of love, and therefore was disconnected from what was going on.

Card 2: the present

The Sun – the Sunflower card falls in the present. It portends happiness and optimism in future relationships. It also suggests that he should shine like the Sun, believing in himself first, as well as his own needs and feelings, rather than creating an illusion of false hopes and expectations. He must live his life to the fullest in order to find fulfillment in any relationship.

Card 3: the future

The Strength – the Allium reveals a wonderful future partnership. It also implies that the querent must control his emotions and stand tall like the Allium. He possesses inner strength and charm, but must first believe in himself and examine what makes him happy. The future indicates that he will achieve this, since he has the inner resolve to heal the past and be confident. Love will undoubtedly make his way to him.

Since all three cards are from the Major Arcana, they show that higher forces are at work and that the past has served as an essential lesson for his own development. Perhaps unsuccessful relationships were unavoidable in some ways – because he needed first to believe in himself and make himself happy, rather than focusing on what he lacked.

1   2   3

The Celtic Cross spread

One of the most common Tarot spreads is the Celtic cross. It covers a wide range of topics while still providing a perspective on a specific situation. In the Celtic Cross spread, ten cards are arranged in the shape of a cross and a staff. The order in which the cards should be laid is indicated in the example on this page.

The meanings of each card position are:

1. The querent – represents the person asking.
2. The obstacle – or challenge to overcome.
3. The root cause – or background of the issue.

querent's fears or concerns about the matter.

8. The environment – around this issue.
9. Hopes and fears – of the querent.
10. The outcome.

3

10

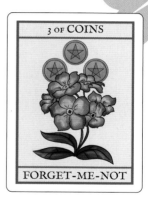

9

5

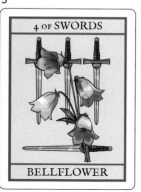

1   2

6

8

4. Recent past – which may have influenced the situation.
5. Advantage / strength – the querent's strength to overcome / resolve this situation.
6. Near future – of the issue in question.
7. Attitude – the

4

7

1

12 THE HANGED MAN

AQUILEGIA

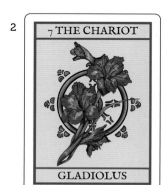

2

7 THE CHARIOT

GLADIOLUS

3

7 OF SWORDS

PHLOX

4

ACE OF WANDS

TULIP

5

4 OF SWORDS

BELLFLOWER

6

2 OF WANDS

BEGONIA

7

KNIGHT OF WANDS

BALSAMINE

8

8 OF CUPS

AZALEA

SAMPLE READING USING THE CELTIC CROSS SPREAD

The querent, a woman in her late forties. After her divorce, she is uncertain about her financial future, going back to work, or starting her own business.

1. The querent: The Hangman – Aquilegia
The first card was chosen at random to represent the querent's current state. Aquilegia, which signifies endurance, encourages her to trust and surrender to her situation. Despite her frustration, stagnation was critical to start her transition and prepare her for her next platform.

2. The obstacles or challenges she has to meet: The Chariot – Gladiolus.
Gladiolus is a resilient flower that bloom in all directions. The message of this card is that the querent has the fortitude and resilience to overcome this challenging phase. Her intuition will guide her, as will her dedication and clear-headedness.

3. The root cause or background to her query: The Seven of Swords – Phlox
This flower represents compatibility, harmony, and oneness. The questioner is advised to be cautious because she has been let down in the past. Desperation can lead to rash actions, which can lead to deception. She is yet to meet the appropriate people who can assist her.

4. The recent past: The Ace of Wands – Tulip.
This card suggests that any recent work or business ideas she had would be fruitful. It also indicates that she has only recently begun a new cycle of growth and inspiration. The vivid red colour of the Tulip represents new optimism and creative ideas.

5. The querent's strength: The Four of Swords – Bellflower.
The Bellflower represents emotional healing, while the Four of Swords represents a need for respite so that healing can occur; otherwise, the querent may become ill from anxiety! This card's message is for the querent to rest and recover. It also symbolizes the end of this stressful period.

9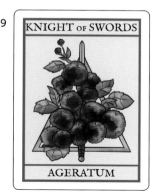

10

6. The near future in relation to the question: The Two of Wands – Begonia.

The Begonia is a delicate flower that represents the unfolding of a potential commercial relationship or partnership. This collaboration could be with someone from another country, or the business will require international collaboration.

7. Fears and concerns of the querent has over her issue: The Knight of Wands – Balsamine.

The Knight of Wands represents vitality and vigour in business. The querent is concerned that she may lack the drive and enthusiasm to start a business or be financially stable. It is, nevertheless, an optimistic card indicating that she will be able to accomplish the future she desires. It also represents a young, business-minded individual who is able to assist her.

8. The environment around the issue: The Eight of Cups – Azalea

This denotes a shift in the querent's emotional state. She has come to the end of her tether. The Azalea is advising her to let go of her problems and take a break in order to gain some perspective. A change of scenery may help her distance herself from her current predicament and gain a new perspective.

9. Hopes and fears of the querent for the future: The Knight of Swords — Ageratum.

The Knight of Swords describes a high-energy persona who makes his presence felt. A full head of

flowering clusters adorns the Ageratum; this card denotes that the querent will have newfound vitality and zest for resuming her life. Her business plans will get off the ground soon.

10. The overall outcome of the matter: The Three of Coins — Forget-Me-Not.

This card indicates that the querent already possesses abilities that will help her achieve financial success. The Forget-Me-Not serves as a reminder of the different skills she already possesses. It assures her of a bright and financially successful future through the use of her abilities, especially when combined with her determination and newfound enthusiasm.

In this reading, there are two major cards that highlight key factors for the querent: the enforced term of suspension is required (card 1), and that she has the inner ability and resources to help her overcome the situation (card 2). The three Swords cards (3, 5, and 9) represent her mental state: stress and concern, whilst the Wands (4, 6, and 7) represent renewed vitality and business ideas. The only Cups card (8) reflects the urge to take a step back and relax. The final card is a Coin card (10), which ensures a positive outcome to her financial inquiry.

THE MAJOR ARCANA

The 22 Major Arcana cards reflect the human psyche and the various stages of our own personal development journey. Starting with The Fool, who is innocent but courageous, each developmental cycle of life takes him to a new level of awareness, honing his abilities and bringing out his unique gifts to fulfil his destiny. The journey ends with the total transformation of The Fool where The World is his oyster.

0 The Fool: Narcissus – New Start. Courage. Adventure.

Keywords: New cycle or project, trust, risk-taking.
Narcissus is associated with rebirth and new beginnings. It symbolizes The Fool at the start of his journey, when he is about to plunge into the unknown. The card signifies both a decision to be made and a new adventure or life cycle. Although you may not be prepared for this new change, the first step requires your courage. New experiences will help you express your full potential and accomplish your life's mission.

1 The Magician: Milfoil – Potential. Talent. Creative Abilities.

Keywords: Skills, potential, mastery, resourcefulness, will, power, creativity, action
This card describes the first lesson. The Fool is learning early in his path that whatever his aims are, he has a natural ability to improve the abilities, skills, and talents that he needs in order to achieve his goals. The clear message of this card is: you have a never-ending source of inspiration, and you are capable of achieving your objectives.

2 The High Priestess: Belladonna – Intuition. Dreams. Spirituality.

Keywords: Spiritual wisdom, intuition, mystery, secrets, hidden knowledge, unseen influences at work, the subconscious and dreams.
The Belladonna flower symbolizes the qualities of The High Priestess: an intuitive, calm woman with hidden knowledge. Someone who is wise and in touch with her subconscious and dreams. This card can also refer to a pregnant woman.

3 The Empress: Lily – Fertility. Abundance. Creativity.

Keywords: Abundance, pleasure, contentment, creativity, nature, nurture, balance, fertility.
The Lily is associated with purity, dedication, and loyalty. The Empress represents inner peace, beauty and abundance, as well as recognizing nature's cycles and living in harmony with it. This card represents timing, the shifting cycles of nature and taking the right action at the right moment for your efforts to bear fruit. It also denotes abundant living and caring for one's physical health and body in order to fulfill one's life's mission. It may also indicate a pregnant woman.

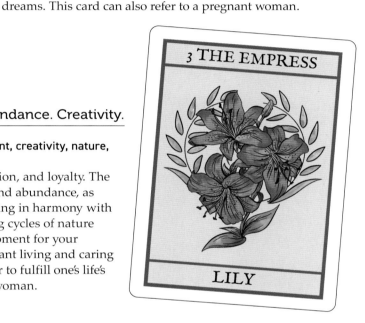

4 The Emperor: Poppy – Power. Structure. Authority.

Keywords: Focus, consistent effort, responsibility, ability, mental clarity or business acumen, satisfaction from achievement.
The Emperor signifies material stability and big worldly achievements that necessitate focus, determination, hard work and dedication. It also indicates the difficulty of adhering to principles and making a solid commitment. The Fool is now challenged to strike a balance between worldly desires and what is important in the long run. The Red Poppy symbolizes an older authoritative gentleman, with mental ability, knowledge and clear thinking. It is a resilient yet delicate flower that represents power, sending a message of caution to be humble and fair and not exploit your authority by acting foolishly.

5 The Hierophant: Tansy – Protection. Destiny. Diplomacy.

Keywords: Religious marriage, tradition, higher purpose, innate wisdom, philosophy, vision.

Tansy means longevity and protection in flower language. It depicts The High Priest, Pope or Hierophant, a natural teacher, diplomat or counsellor from whom you might seek advice. It describes a wise person, someone who has knowledge and deeper wisdom and applies it to make his vision a reality. When this card appears in a spread, it indicates that one's destiny is about to be fulfilled or that a religious marriage ceremony will take place if it appears with the Lovers card.

6 The Lovers: Rose – Passion. Courage. Union.

Keywords: Partnerships — romantic or business, love, collaboration with others, harmony between opposites, making a choice.

This card signifies a harmonious union of two people, as well as the courage to be one's genuine self in order to find true love (or the right partner). The rose is strong and attractive but it has a thorny stem, which warns the querent to make the proper choice when choosing a partner. If it occurs alongside The Hierophant, it can represent a religious marriage, or civil ceremony if the Justice card also appears within the same spread.

7 The Chariot: Gladiolus – Mastery. Integrity. Victory.

Keywords: Conflict, control, discipline, strength, stability, willpower, effort, triumph.

At this point in life, you must be practical and regularly apply your developed skills as well as mental focus in order to overcome any problem or struggle you may be experiencing. This card represents triumph. The Gladiolus is a hardy flower that blossoms in every direction and encourages you to keep going. Your efforts are about to be rewarded, and fresh presents are on the way.

8 Strength: Allium – Compassion. Self-control. Healing.

Keywords: Elegance, beauty, strength, control, confidence, balance, integrity, courage, generosity, compassion.

This card signifies a higher level of insight and the ability to control one's own primal forces. The Fool, like the Allium flower, is called to master his dualism and seek a deeper understanding of instincts. Stand tall and elegantly in the face of hardship; you have a natural ability to heal it and transform the circumstance to your favour. Better times are on the way! This is your chance to prove your inner strength and wisdom. You will prevail over life's hardships if you have the fortitude to endure.

9 The Hermit: Lavender – Wisdom. Learning. Solitude.

Keywords: Withdrawal, detachment, patience, travel, seeking knowledge.

The lavender blossom is unassuming in appearance, but its aroma reaches a great distance. This card invites you to retire into solitude in order to think on and learn from your experiences thus far. The wisdom of life's challenges will be revealed if you take time off to contemplate, like The Hermit who withdraws to reflect and understand. You will have a deeper understanding of your life and be able to share this knowledge with others, enlightening them.

10 WHEEL OF FORTUNE

CLOVER

10 Wheel of Fortune: Clover – Luck. Success. The Unexpected.

Keywords: Luck, chance, fortune, quick change, new direction.
The Clover symbolizes a sudden and unexpected change of fortune. Influences that can change the outcome of a current circumstance. It could signal new opportunities or a cycle in life, for example. Regardless of the current constraints, this card represents a breakthrough or unexpected swift changes, such as moving residences, meeting someone new or obtaining a job offer — depending on where it falls in a spread.

11 Justice: Iris – Fortitude. Prudence. Agreement.

Keywords: Fairness, impartiality, balance, harmony between opposing forces, decision, equality, truth.
The Iris flower reflects the qualities of Justice. Its colours are perfectly balanced, resulting in harmony. The message of this card is that when opposing forces are in harmony, the appropriate decision can be taken; nonetheless, choices have consequences since they cause change. You are advised to consider that making the right decision requires a dispassionate evaluation of your situation, using your intellect and facts – not emotions. The situation requires you to be honest and fair.

11 JUSTICE

IRIS

12 THE HANGED MAN

AQUILEGIA

13 DEATH

ACONITE

12 The Hanged Man: Aquilegia – Trust. Surrender. Transformation.

Keywords: Sacrifice, patience, waiting, surrender, enlightenment, trust, maturity.

The Aquilegia flower represents endurance. It is inviting you to make a deliberate decision to freely to let go of the past (self or habits), which opens up the possibility of gaining something better. This card depicts a period of suspension and delay required to prepare for a new cycle of rejuvenation. You can overcome the cause of your delay by trusting your higher knowledge and letting go of old habits and beliefs.

13 Death: Aconite – End. New beginning. Transformation.

Keywords: Endings, loss, mourning, acceptance, adjustment, change, transition, rebirth, renewal.

Because of its dual characteristics, Aconite was employed throughout the Middle Ages: it can poison and kill or cure and restore health. As it heralds a fresh beginning, this card confirms the permanent end of the old ways. It teaches The Fool that the old ways are doomed and that he must change. He is transformed as he comes to terms with loss. According to its position in a spread, death might represent a change of relationship or home.

14 Temperance: Chrysanthemum – Balance. Healing. Resolution.

Keywords: Balanced temperament, respite, moderation, negotiation, cooperation, compromise, adaptability.
This card indicates a brief break from life's difficulties. The Fool has learnt to manage his thoughts (The Emperor, The Chariot) and feelings (Strength) and can now relate harmoniously with others. The key to resolving any conflict is to make a compromise. If this card appears in a spread with The Lovers card, it suggests a lovely relationship or reaching an accord with others.

15 The Devil: Orchid – Temptation. Obsession. Restriction.

Keywords: Being stuck, lust, greed, rage, primal instincts.
The Devil card does not reflect evil in any way. It forces The Fool to confront the murky, instinctive side of himself that is inhibiting his development. It symbolizes voluntarily confining oneself to unconscious fears, greed or desires. This card represents an imbalanced attachment to a relationship that is not serving our highest good, or being imprisoned by our concerns and desires when it appears in a spread. The card represents progress and liberation through opting to break free from such attachments.

16 The Tower: Venus Flytrap – Eruption. Upheaval. Inescapable.

Keywords: Sudden upheaval, conflict, disruption, quick enforced change.

Venus Flytraps, as the name suggests, trap insects, leaving them unable to escape! The Tower depicts a sudden eruption, a crisis that cannot be avoided. It calls for the eradication of past beliefs and ways of life. The Tower card causes The Fool to reconsider the decisions he has made thus far on his voyage. Simultaneously, the rapid destruction of the old structures allows for building a new, more suitable foundation for his personal development.

17 The Star: Lotus – Bliss. Determination. Renewal.

Keywords: Hope, faith, inspiration, fulfilled wishes, healing, new horizons.

As its petals open one by one, the lotus flower represents healing, meditation and renewal. This card represents optimism and ascension to higher spiritual levels through emotional experiences. The Fool is through a rebirth and must not give up on his dreams; his wishes are about to be granted. This is a great time to reflect on what is actually important. There is hope for the future, and healing is possible. You are ready to both give and receive love.

18 The Moon: Calla Lily – Wisdom. Unconscious. Illusion.

Keywords: Intuition, dreams, unconscious fears, confusion, deception, disillusionment.
The petal of the Calla Lily wraps around its pistil until the moment comes to unveil it. The Moon is related to the night and represents darkness, confusion and a lack of clarity. However, as the Moon cycles change over time, the truth will be revealed through intuition or dreams. This card indicates hidden issues, unspoken anxieties and guidance through dreams.

19 The Sun: Sunflower – Optimism. Longevity. Success.

Keywords: Joy, optimism, clarity, success, ambition, opportunity, vibrant health, vitality.
The Sunflower grows and nurtures its vibrant colour by always facing the sun! This card signifies the best moment to take advantage of opportunities and live life to the fullest. The Sun rises above The Fool after the Moon's gloom and uncertainty, signifying clarity of thought, fresh birth, fruition, successful pursuits, happiness and renewed vitality.

20 Judgement: Everlasting – Permanent Transformation. Turning Point.

Keywords: Reward for past effort, re-evaluation, responsibility, outcome, resolution, acceptance.

Every action we take in life has long-term ramifications. This card reflects The Fool's last evaluation of his development, wisdom and maturity. After being stripped of his ego (Death) and his possessions (Tower), he is ready to be reborn to a new beginning, his true and larger purpose. It denotes an inescapable positive shift, even though it appears to be unfavourable.

21 The World: Lily of the Valley – Happiness. Joy. Fulfilment.

Keywords: integration, fulfilment, achievement, completion, ending, final reward, success.

This is the final stage of The Fool's development into his full potential. This card signifies successful goal achievement, fame, harmony and fulfilment, just as the rich green leaves of the Lily of the Valley cover the delicate white petals until they are ready to emerge. The Fool has achieved equilibrium, having completely balanced many polarities within himself — the world is his!

THE MINOR ARCANA

While the Major Arcana cards deal with life's major events, the Minor Arcana cards deal with day-to-day activities, events and people in our lives, as well as sentiments, our thinking and experiences that have a short-term impact on us.

The Minor Arcana consists of four suits: Wands, Cups, Swords and Coins. Each suit can be viewed as a voyage or cycle, beginning with the ace and ascending numerically to ten, followed by the court cards.

The Court Cards

The Tarot deck has 16 court cards, with a king, queen, knight and page for each of the four suits. If a court card appears in a spread, it may indicate a person in the querent's life who possesses the card's specific characteristics. It can also symbolize the querent's attributes that need to be expressed.

The Kings are mature male authority figures who exemplify power, accomplishment and responsibility. Queens are mature, maternal ladies who, like kings, wield power. They represent wisdom, assurance, fertility and life-giving abilities.

Knights are younger men and women who represent people, characteristics or personality types, or a change and movement in a new direction. Pages are children or young teenagers of any gender who represent youthful promise, dreams and other traits based on the suit to which they belong. They embody sensitive qualities that must be nourished if they are to develop. Pages are messengers who indicate when and where news of some type will be received, as well as times and seasons of the year.

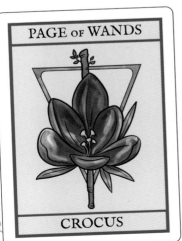

PAGE OF WANDS

CROCUS

ACE OF WANDS

TULIP

WANDS

The Wands court cards represent people with brown/auburn colouring. Wands are associated with the fire element and the spring season. They represent life force, growth, travel, intuition, job, business and hope for the future.

In the Flower Tarot, Wands cards are a swirl of brilliant colours in full blossom, ready to burst forth into their full potential. They indicate activity that frequently manifests as action – sometimes creative, sometimes protective or sometimes hostile. A spread with a large number of Wands suggests that things are moving quickly.

Ace of Wands: Tulip – Growth of New Ideas.

This card signifies a new adventure or endeavour, which could be sparked by a new job or relationship. Like the petals of a Tulip, the experience opens and takes shape as it begins. It refers to the birth of a child in the family. Decide what you want, since the moment has come for it to bloom.

Two of Wands: Begonia – Balanced Business Partnerships.

Now is the moment to move forward after giving birth to a new concept or beginning. Your strategy has been defined; seek assistance and support to see it through to completion. Your efforts will begin to bloom once they have taken root.

Three of Wands: Cornflower – Collaboration. Success. Expansion.

Prosperity shines as brightly as this cornflower! This card foretells of impending success. Now is the time to start planning for the future. Expansion into other markets, fame and acknowledgement are also on the horizon.

Four of Wands: Garden Sage – Joy. Attainment. Stability.

The message of this card is a cheerful one! Happy times are here. The Garden Sage foretells of a time of stability and celebration, such as births, weddings or anniversaries. It also indicates the querent's wish to live affluently.

Five of Wands: Pale Smartweed – Adjustments. Negotiation. Arguments.

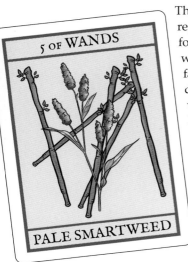

The Pale Smartweed represents the necessity for devotion and hard work. You may be facing serious financial difficulties, but you will be helped. So, keep at it, weed out the obstacles, and your efforts will finally bear fruit. Conflict can be avoided.

Six of Wands: Muscari – Stability. Achievement. Victory.

The Muscari flower is a harbinger of good fortune in your pursuits. The abundant blossom stems of this plant represent financial security, conquering past challenges, and receiving recognition for your work. There's some exciting news on the way!

Seven of Wands: Galanthus – Choices. Disagreements. Perseverance.

The splendour of the Galanthus bloom symbolizes your reward for your perseverance. You may be in a disagreement with others, but you have the advantage. Be fair while maintaining control of the issue and applying pressure. You will leverage your competitive instincts to protect yourself and your creative initiatives.

Eight of Wands: Fuchsia – Travel. Movement. Development.

The vibrant Fuchsia colours express the message of the Eight of Wands: your perseverance and hard work are about to be rewarded. Business transactions and projects will proceed smoothly. There is the possibility of a fruitful international connection.

Nine of Wands: Marigold – Strength. Reflection. Flexibility.

The warm yellow colours of the Marigold flower evoke the wisdom and inspiration represented by the Nine of Wands: it is time to put the struggle down and consider the best course of action. If you want to reach your objectives, you must be willing to adapt and to rethink your strategy.

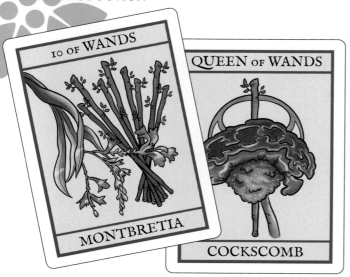

Ten of Wands: Montbretia – Progression. Rest. Recharge.

The red Montbretia of the Ten of Wands warns you against engaging in immature behaviour at this time, as it is the right moment to maintain your efforts. Your aspirations are enormous, so take it gradually. Continue in a responsible manner. When you put too much strain on yourself, your physical health will suffer.

Page of Wands: Crocus – Energetic. Restless. Warm.

The Page of Wands depicts a youngster who is lively, warm and creative, but who is also hyperactive. The arrival of the blue Crocus heralds the beginning of Spring, a period of frenetic activity, fresh beginnings, inspiration and creativity. So, make sensible decisions going forwards, and you will harvest what you sow.

Knight of Wands: Balsamine – Foreign Business Connections.

Another name for Balsamine is Touch-Me-Not and this name hints at the Knight's temperament – while bold, charming and daring, there is trouble afoot if his temper gets the better of him. Often this indicates that you can take a risk with a venture abroad at this time.

Queen of Wands: Cockscomb – Kind. Enthusiastic. Loyal.

Cockscomb embodies the Queen of Wands in all her radiance: she is a fearless, smart lady who is autonomous and authoritative, creative, perceptive, strong and daring. She understands exactly what she wants and how to obtain it. The Queen of Wands, like the Cockscomb flower, cannot be overlooked! This card also indicates the traits or attributes that you need to cultivate in yourself.

King of Wands: Hyacinth – Successful. Tolerant. Calm.

The King of Wands is a powerful, mature visionary with excellent leadership characteristics. He relies on his wisdom and intuition to guide his decision-making, particularly in business. He has an effect on others around him, just the way the aroma of hyacinth fills the room it is in. The King is vivacious and full of energy, and lives life to the fullest. The card depicts a man you know with these characteristics, or it may signal skills you need to improve.

CUPS

Cups signify sentiments, love, relationships, and emotional fulfilment. They relate to the element of water; and represent our imagination as well as our unconscious. They depict fair-haired individuals, pleasure and psychic activity.

Water quenches our thirst. So, when our cup is full it indicates fulfilment. But, occasionally the water is spilt, indicating crisis and sadness. Sometimes, it overflows expressing a trauma or grief. Several Cup cards in a spread call for paying attention to our emotional state or relationships. They also indicate news of births, marriages or falling in love.

Ace of Cups: Peony – Bliss. Healing. Happiness.

The Peony is typically offered on important occasions as a gesture of goodwill, best wishes and joy. It is symbolic of love, honour, happiness, wealth, romance and beauty. The Ace of Cups represents a start of a new relationship, pregnancy or childbirth, or a marriage proposal if The Lovers card is present with either The Hierophant or Justice in the same spread. It signifies deep emotional happiness, fulfilment and joy.

Two of Cups: Pansy – Harmony. Loyal. Partnerships

Pansy represents loving feelings. You can offer Pansy flowers to almost anyone who means a lot to you. The Two of Cups represents a romantic relationship, a marriage, or a close friendship. It portrays harmony in romantic and plutonic partnerships and the fruition of your creative projects.

Three of Cups: Aster – Collaboration. Birth. Marriage.

Aster is the flower of love and honour. The Three of Cups represents a joyful celebration signalling wonderful news such as a pregnancy, a marriage proposal or achievement in a creative project close to your heart. Be proud of your accomplishments but humble and grounded. Excessive indulgence or exaggerated emotional display, however, may result in disharmony or imbalance.

Four of Cups: Primrose – Boredom. Disappointment. Re-evaluation.

You are in the midst of a personal crisis, and wondering if your loved ones will stand by you. However, The Primrose calls you to reconsider your priorities and you will be inspired in the right direction. Something better is on the way.

Five of Cups: Daisy – Loss. Revival. Cheerfulness.

You have suffered a loss, yet the bright colour of the Daisy flower promises good cheer and healing. The Five of Cups represents a loss, but it is not a total loss; you may still recover and rebuild on what is left.

Six of Cups: Purslane – Kinship. Affinity. Innocence.

This is a period of tranquility following an emotional storm. You will experience joy and childlike happiness. Perhaps an old friend with whom you have lost contact will re-appear, bringing a fresh new perspective on your life. New friendships can form as well. Hope for the future will be rekindled.

Seven of Cups: Anemone – Choices. Foresight. Caution.

The Seven of Cups represents the need to be grounded when deciding. Anemone is thought to bring good fortune and to ward off evil. It signals a warning: not everything that glitters is gold. Unless you remain practical and realistic, your dreams may become an illusion.

Eight of Cups: Azalea –Letting Go. Shift. Self-Love.

Azaleas represent a longing for home and wishing to return to it. The Eight of Cups is urging you back to yourself, to cultivate what truly offers you happiness, and to walk away from unsatisfactory emotional ties that have taken their toll on you.

Nine of Cups: Dandelion – Fulfilment. Joy. Attainment.

The Dandelion is a humble flower that symbolizes growth, hope and healing. It represents the Nine of Cups, which encourages you to be modest while your desires are granted. Your dedication and hard work are going to be rewarded.

Ten of Cups: Cosmos – Special Event. Marriage. Lasting Happiness.

The Cosmos flower symbolizes calm and order, and it has romantic meaning. It promises your partner that the two of you will journey through life together. It depicts the Ten of Cups, which indicates a cycle of long-term happiness, emotional fulfilment, marriage or children.

Page of Cups: Nemophila – Imagination. Poetic. Emotional.

In floral language, Nemophila signifies 'success everywhere'. The Page of Cups has a sensitive, caring nature and is easily hurt. This card encourages you to pursue your creative side rather than being lazy or spending your day daydreaming! Act now to make your aspirations a reality.

Knight of Cups: Tobacco – Sensitive. Creative. Dreamer.

KNIGHT OF CUPS

TOBACCO

The Knight of Cups is a young man who is poetic, compassionate and romantic; often depicting fair-haired males. Tobacco has rich appealing green leaves and lovely blooms that carry nicotine with an arousing warning: although you may appreciate the romance, be careful not to be led astray with this romantic type.

Queen of Cups: Magnolia – Artistic. Intuitive. Graceful.

Magnolia symbolizes The Queen of Cups, who is feminine, artistic, creative and empathetic, and it is also a symbol of dignity and perseverance. She is a wonderful listener and delivers sound advice. Over-perseverance, on the other hand, could lead to codependency and a victim-mindset.

King of Cups: Dahlia - Mature. Balanced. Charismatic.

This card represents an elderly gentleman who is mature, kind and well-balanced. The King of Cups is devoted, gregarious and open about his emotions. Dahlias have deep significance in flower language representing wealth, elegance and loyalty in love. However, in Victorian England, red dahlias symbolized betrayal and dishonesty – traits of a flawed King of Cups!

SWORDS

Swords represent ideas, thoughts, worry, worries, sadness or loss and the element of air. Their blades are double-edged, suggesting that any decision you make may have both positive and negative implications. The court cards represent people with dark hair and a dark complexion, with mental abilities.

ACE OF SWORDS

DELPHINIUM

Ace of Swords: Delphinium – Obstacles. Decision. New Beginning.

The Ace of Swords represents strong forces and difficulties. 'You have the strength to overcome problems,' says the Delphinium's cheering message. It is a period of decision-making and transitioning into a new direction.

Two of Swords: Coneflower – Decision. Tension. Justice.

The Two of Swords describes a tense situation, which you are seeking to balance but failing. To alleviate the tension, a difficult but sensible decision must be made. The Coneflower conveys a message of healing and health: make the choice, otherwise worrying will cause your health to suffer.

Three of Swords: Zinnia – Separation. Quarrels. Loss.

In problems of the heart, this card represents sorrow and disappointment. A separation of some sort is possible. The Zinnia flower serves as a reminder to recognize our emotional needs and not take emotional happiness for granted.

Four of Swords: Bellflower – Rest. Pause. End of Troubles.

The Four of Swords provides relief from a difficult situation. The Bellflower conveys a message of hope and gratitude: things may have been worse, but the worst is behind us. A rest or a vacation is required to recover; otherwise, physical health may suffer.

Five of Swords: Carnation - Troubles. Lies. Gossip.

Carnations represent deep grief, sudden loss or repossession. This card denotes unfair play and abusive behaviour against you. Although you won, your success brings you as much grief as it does your opponents. However, it was impossible to avoid the situation.

Six of Swords: Gazania – Ease. Flow. Travel.

This card represents water travel, a vacation away from difficulties; peace will be restored. The Gazania's message is one of wealth and abundance. A new chapter of joy and stability is about to begin.

Seven of Swords: Phlox – Deception. Prudence. Caution.

The Phlox represents wisdom and protection against deception. The Seven of Swords advises you to be cautious in a certain situation, or you may be duped. Some of the options available to you are deceptive.

Eight of Swords: Henbane – Stalemate. Trapped. Stuck.

This card represents a stalemate situation; you are stuck and cannot see a way out. The Henbane flower delivers a spiritual message to wait for inspiration: now is not the time for hasty decisions or rash action.

Nine of Swords: Calendula – Oppression. Anxiety. Distress.

Calendula was a Victorian metaphor for grief, despair and sorrow. This card denotes a lot of tension and suffering. Your problems are causing you so much mental anguish that you're losing sleep and most likely having nightmares. Take care of your mental health. You might start to think differently and see a way out if you accept the situation. Before you can let go of the past, you must accept your limitations.

Ten of Swords: Hemlock – Treachery. Deception. Force.

This card signifies both sorrow and joy. You are at the end of a bad cycle. Life can only get better! Distress can be transformed into joy by shifting your mental attitude. Lessons have been learnt; and you will move forward with a new perspective and a better understanding of yourself and the situation.

Page of Swords: Gillyflower – Sportive. Difficult. Bright.

A clever, witty but difficult child is symbolized by this card. His actions might be rash, but he is inquisitive and quick to learn. It symbolizes honing abilities and skills for your advancement.

Knight of Swords: Ageratum – Assertive. Forceful. Decisive.

This card describes a courageous warrior who fights for justice. However, his immediate reaction is always to fight! It suggests a personality trait, or a skilled person, whose presence is felt but whose actions are untimely and inappropriate to the situation. In this case, attack may not be the best defence!

Queen of Swords: Hortensia – Strong-Minded. Lonely. Conqueror.

Hortensia is associated with The Queen of Swords and represents appreciation, grace and beauty. It denotes a graceful person or personality with exceptional mental abilities. Someone who was able to overcome their difficulties via clear thinking and sensible action.

King of Swords: Lupin – Logical. Strategist. Shrewd.

Lupin derived its name from the Latin word for wolf. It was originally thought that the flower absorbed all of the nutrients from the soil. In reality, it provides much-needed nitrogen. As The King of Swords, it symbolizes a quick-witted, logical and clever man. Someone who is a good judge of character or situation, and who possesses attributes that the querent should cultivate in order to resolve a situation.

COINS

Coins or pentacles represent matter, the body, finances, skills and the physical world; physical well-being and the opportunity to find comfort in personal possessions. They represent money, skills, talents or business savvy needed to earn a living and contribute to society in a meaningful way. The Court cards symbolize dark-haired or dark-skinned people.

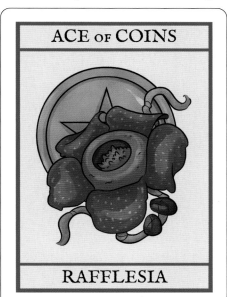

Ace of Coins: Rafflesia – Prosperity. Receiving Money.

The Rafflesia is an unusual large flower thought to capture insects. The Ace of Coins signifies a new chance or endeavour that you must seize upon and put your talents to work on. It can also signify receiving a significant sum of money.

Two of Coins: Godetia – Two Incomes. Financial Success.

Godetia represents vivacity and charm. This card's message suggests that you now have the opportunity to generate two streams of income to balance your finances. You're ready, so, go for it!

Five of Coins: Nasturtium – Financial Problems. Change Mind-set.

You are now experiencing financial difficulties and anticipate the worst! However, Nasturtium, which represents conquest, sends a message of hope and reassurance: you are capable of restoring your finances or finding work if you have recently lost one. Your abilities, efforts and hard work will be rewarded.

Six of Coins: Petunia – Generosity. Justice. Sharing.

Your generous personality is described by the soothing Petunia flower. You have achieved your financial objectives and are sharing your good fortune with others. Share your fortune as you celebrate with others. Giving time and money to excellent causes gives a lot of satisfaction.

Seven of Coins: Geranium - Fortitude. Don't Give Up.

Geranium radiates optimism and good wishes. You have a difficult period ahead of you, but don't give up! You should not lose faith, but rather, after a short break, pick yourself up and make the necessary modifications.

Three of Coins: Forget-me-not – Collaboration. Joint Ventures.

Forget-me-not symbolizes mutual admiration and respect. This card describes the qualities and skills you possess that will lead to your success. Joint ventures or company collaborations with others will be a success if you consider them. Financial matters will flourish.

Four of Coins: Gerbera Daisy – Financial Security.

The most notable feature of this flower is its vivid, luminous colours, which are associated with energy and regeneration. Financial matters are your priority at the moment, and you are well positioned to succeed in all financial matters. Remember to set aside money for savings and also reinvest money to grow your business.

8 OF COINS

CHAMOMILE

Eight of Coins: Chamomile – Patience. New Project. Reward.

This card denotes learning a new skill or taking on a new undertaking. You are polishing your talents in preparation for a new project that will be demanding. Financial success, on the other hand, is indicated. Stay calm, and trust your abilities. You're on the right path.

Nine of Coins: Gold Poppy – Material Success. Windfall. Retirement.

Life is wonderful! You are going to enter a new era of your life in which you have achieved financial security to the point where you no longer need to work. This card indicates that your work and dedication are soon to be rewarded.

Ten of Coins: Lilac – Renewal. Financial Comfort.

You will become accustomed to luxurious living, but be careful not to become lazy and over-indulgent. Lilac brings you hope and sound advice. This card indicates that long-term prosperity and material happiness have been attained. You are comfortable in your home and may leave a positive legacy to your descendants.

Page of Coins: Bergenia – Profit. Studious. Financial Mind.

This card describes or characterizes a young person who is studious or financially minded, and indicates small winnings if you have started a project recently.

The Knight of Coins: Clematis – Methodical. Reliable. Logical.

This flower represents mental beauty and inventiveness! It represents a young dark-haired man who is rational, methodical and steady in his approach and in whom you can put your trust. If it occurs reversed in a reading, it represents someone who cannot be trusted with money or who has financial troubles.

Queen of Coins: Mallow – Supportive. Practical. Wealthy.

In flower language, the Mallow represents love, protection and health. It defines a well-off, helpful, practical and supportive grown lady who may also be a professional or business-minded person. The Queen of Coins would be a fantastic business mentor.

King of Coins: Houseleek – Wealthy. Financial Security. Honest.

Houseleek is supposed to protect the home from fire and lightning, as well as keep the family safe and prosperous. It refers to an older, mature man on whom you can rely. He is compassionate, self-made and extremely successful or affluent in business. He is helpful, but he has high standards for others.

KING OF COINS

HOUSELEEK

8 OF WANDS
FUCHSIA

4 THE EMPER...
POPPY

THE CARDS

NOW COLOUR AND CUT OUT YOUR TAROT CARD DECK.
IF YOU LIKE, YOU CAN USE THE IMAGES ON THIS PAGE AS A GUIDE,
OR SIMPLY CHOOSE FROM YOUR OWN PERSONAL COLOUR PALETTE.

7 OF SWORDS
PHLOX

4 OF CUPS
PRIMROS...

ACE OF WANDS
TULIP

6 OF COINS
PETUNIA

12 THE HANGED MAN
AQUILEGIA

6 OF CUPS
PURSLANE

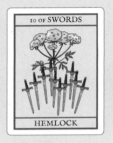

10 OF SWORDS
HEMLOCK

14 TEMPERA...
CHRYSANTHE...

5 OF SWORDS
CARNATION

9 OF SWORDS
CALENDULA

3 OF WANDS
CORNFLOWER

5 THE HIEROPHANT
TANSY

KING OF SWORDS
LUPIN

ACE OF CU...
PEONY

15 THE DEVIL
ORCHID

10 OF WANDS
MONTBRETIA

6 OF SWORDS
GAZANIA

KING OF COINS
HOUSELEEK

19 THE SUN
SUNFLOWER

5 OF CUPS
DAISY

ACE OF COINS
RAFFLESIA

3 THE EMPRESS
LILY

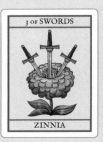

3 OF SWORDS
ZINNIA

20 JUDGMENT
EVERLASTING

KING OF WANDS
HYACINTH

21 THE WOR...
LILY OF THE VA...